pocket
cornwall

Seal Secrets:
Cornwall and the Isles of Scilly

Sue Sayer

Alison Hodge

First published in 2012 by Alison Hodge,
2 Clarence Place, Penzance, Cornwall TR18
2QA, UK info@alison-hodge.co.uk
www.alisonhodgepublishers.co.uk

Reprinted 2013

ISBN-13 978-0-906720-84-4

British Library Cataloguing-in-Publication Data
A catalogue record for this book is available from
the British Library.

Designed and originated by BDP – Book Design
and Production, Penzance, Cornwall

Printed in China

Acknowledgements

I should like to thank my many friends in
Cornwall Seal Group, and all our partner
organizations, who are a constant source
of inspiration, encouragement and support;
James Barnett and Dave Jarvis for proof-
reading and checking my draft for factual
accuracy; and my partner, Chris, for his
unfailing patience and tolerance of my
obsession with grey seals.

For permission to reproduce photographs,
I am grateful to: Keith Hiscock (page 36,
right); Terry Hocking (hooded seal, page 11),
Dave McBride (pages 16, 61, 67), and Sue
Waterhouse (page 63, bottom).

Contents

Introduction

'Upside-down V plane'

Cornwall's most frequently sighted and iconic marine mammals, grey seals are creatures whose lives connect and bind together our terrestrial and marine worlds. The margin between our land and sea environment is exposed to the rawest and toughest conditions in nature: welcome to the world of the grey seal! One of the rarest seal species on our planet, but common around the coasts of Cornwall and the Isles of Scilly, grey seals are both powerful and stunning; their resilient yet flexibly sleek bodies glisten as they dance through the white water of our most awesome winter breakers. In a quiet, reflective moment as I sit on a cliff top on a calmer, sunny day, the inquisitive nature of a grey seal becomes apparent as it glances up curiously, making eye contact with me, before crash-diving mischievously to create a huge, loud splash.

I cannot remember when I first saw a grey seal, nor when I fell in love with them, developing a passion that has become an inspiring focus in my life. I would have seen grey seals during my annual Scottish holidays as a child, but it was my first pair of binoculars that transformed my passing interest into enthusiastic obsession. In this magnified, circular world, I saw seals emerge from the sea for the first time and was rewarded with close-up views of them going about their daily lives, almost as if I was among them. I was hooked. I hope to share some of their secrets with you.

Sue Sayer
2012

About this Book

'Mowgli' the seal pup

Photos of cute, white-coated seal pups conceal the harsh realities of their lives. This book provides a glimpse of the hidden and secret world of the grey seals of Cornwall and the Isles of Scilly from 'cradle to grave'.

Deliberately written from the perspective of an observational researcher, who has spent far too many hours watching seals in the wild in Cornwall and the Isles of Scilly, it is hoped that this book will provide a unique

Sue (left), with the Cornwall Seal Group Steering Committee – Kate and Dan

insight into the private and often surprising lives of our grey seals. It includes real stories about individual wild seals. (These stories are told in *italics*.)

Anthropomorphizing is not encouraged by the scientific community, but I use it here to illustrate and describe seal behaviour, and to create more vibrant images. When watching seals, my aim is to try to understand the motivation behind their hugely varied behaviour and interactions. To eliminate such descriptions would greatly diminish the richness of the social interactivity of this highly developed and intelligent marine creature.

When I started trying to recognize individual seals, I would sit on the cliff top, drawing their fur patterns that I could see through my binoculars. This was a painstaking process, but a good way to imprint the fur patterns in my brain. Most seals have been named after the pictures I see in their fur patterns.

The invention of digital photography and eight-gigabyte SD memory cards has been revolutionary, making the capture of hundreds of photographs of an individual seal from different angles possible and affordable.

I have spent thousands of hours at exposed sites, literally in all weathers, observing seals, but always at distance. Observation must be remote for seal behaviour to be natural and unmodified by my presence. Most of the photographs in this book have been taken from cliff tops by digiscoping – using a compact camera attached to a telescope, enabling magnifications rarely achievable through affordable SLR cameras.

For more information about my work, please visit **www.cornwallsealgroup.co.uk**, or email **sue@cornwallsealgroup.co.uk**.

Note: The word 'Cornwall' is used in this book for brevity, and refers to Cornwall and the Isles of Scilly.

Spotting the Special Seals of the South West of Britain

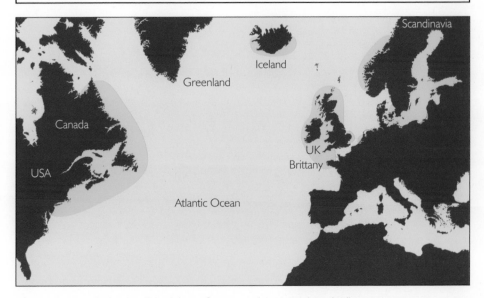

Grey seals live on both sides of the Atlantic Ocean – in the areas coloured yellow

Britain's largest land-breeding marine mammals, grey seals (*Halichoerus grypus*) inhabit our wildest and most exposed rocky shores, loving the sensation of stormy white water, the primitive echoes of dark sea caves, and the seclusion of remote sandy beaches. Their proper title is the North Atlantic grey seal, describing their range which extends from the eastern seaboard of the USA and Canada across the North Atlantic to western

Seal in a harbour

effective protection and maintenance of grey seal habitats in Cornwall is critical for future generations of these unique creatures across the Celtic fringe.

Where to see grey seals in Cornwall

Europe from Scandinavia in the north, down to a southern limit of north-west France. Between one-third and one-half of all the world's grey seals live in UK waters, and 90 per cent of these are in Scotland. Cornwall is at the hub of a genetically distinct sub-population of Celtic seals, which move north to south-west Ireland and Wales, and south to France. This makes the grey seals in Cornwall very special indeed. Tolerance of such varied environmental conditions demonstrates the grey seal's adaptability, giving hope for its continued survival during global warming. Rising sea levels, however, will significantly affect their haul-out and breeding sites, making their survival more questionable. The

Grey seals can be seen all around the Cornish coast, and in the Isles of Scilly. Of marine mammals, grey seals are unique in that they spend extended periods of time on land and may dry out fully with no ill effects. While on land, however, grey seals are extremely vulnerable, and for this reason the geographical locations of haul-out and breeding sites have been omitted from this book in order to protect seals from ever-increasing levels of anthropogenic disturbance. To get close to seals, visit the National Seal Sanctuary at Gweek, where you will get better views of them than in the wild. Many boat trips to see seals are advertised widely in the local media, departing from Looe, Penzance, St Mary's in the Isles of Scilly, St Ives and Newquay, but note that seals are most likely to be seen around low tide. At high tide, good views of wild grey seals can be experienced

Boat trip to see seals

in harbours, particularly in St Ives and New-quay. But please read the chapter on Threats to Seals (pages 66–72) to understand why it is essential that seals are never fed in the wild, because doing so has many detrimental effects on their well-being.

Seal Species in Cornwall

An adult common, or harbour, seal (in front) with a juvenile grey seal (behind)

Most seals around our coast are grey seals, but we do get other, vagrant species. Common or harbour seals (*Phocina vitulina*) are being identified with increasing frequency, so it pays to know the differences between these and the more numerous grey seals.

All sightings of these seals should be reported to Seaquest South West via the Cornwall Wildlife Trust's website, which is listed on page 80.

Grey seals are the larger and stronger of the two species, while common seals benefit

A hooded seal

from greater athletic agility. Common seals tend to have a mottled fur pattern, creating perfect camouflage for sheltered, bladder wrack-covered rocky shores. Grey seals may be plain, or blotched and spotty. The easiest way to distinguish between them is to look carefully at their heads. In proportion to their bodies, common seals have relatively small heads, with clear foreheads down to their shorter snouts and snub noses. From the front, their heads are rounded and the nostrils form a distinct 'v' shape. Grey seals have much larger heads, with strong, flat-profiled snouts, which become more Romanesque as they get older. From the front, grey seals' heads form a vertical oval shape; their nostrils (except in juveniles) are much more parallel. Common seals' heads appear more cat-like; grey seals' heads are more dog-like.

Other seal species seen in Cornish waters come from the Arctic: the hooded seal (*Cystophora cristata*) and the harp seal (*Pagophilus groenlandicus*). It is interesting that when one species has appeared in Cornwall, so has the other. Both are spectacular species, but very different from each other. Hooded seals, which are slightly bigger than grey seals, are named after the balloon-like appendages that males can inflate on top of their noses. Adult harp seals are smaller, and have a distinctive dark band that begins in a point at the front and top of the back and extends diagonally down both sides towards the rear flippers. Harp seal pups are the main focus for Canadian seal hunters. Sightings of these seal species should also always be reported to Seaquest South West via the Cornwall Wildlife Trust's website, listed on page 80.

Adaptations to Life on Land and in the Sea

A seal's webbed rear flippers and tail

Grey seals share a common ancestry with cats, dogs, otters and bears, and have characteristics in common with each of them. They are long-lived mammals, with males thought to live to 25 years old in the wild and females to over 30 years old; the oldest recorded wild female grey seal lived to 46 years. In captivity, one of the oldest recorded grey seals achieved the grand old age of 40 years – this was Magnus, who spent the last 18 years of his life at the National Seal Sanctuary at Gweek.

Grey seals are streamlined for life at sea, using alternating sideways movements of their powerful rear flippers to propel them through the water. At speed, their fore-flippers are folded tight against their sides and a small tail acts as a rudder. Once out of the water and moving or hauling across land, a seal's fore-flippers become the principal driving force of locomotion. Powerful shoulders throw both fore-flippers in front of the seal's body with strong claws adding grip, as muscle movements ripple through the seal's

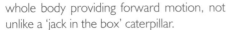
Clockwise from top left: A seal moving at speed

whole body providing forward motion, not unlike a 'jack in the box' caterpillar.

Often described as ungainly on land, grey seals can move surprising quickly, and can outrun all but the fastest adult human! It is at the junction of land and sea that a seal's marine instinct and terrestrial dexterous strength become apparent. Once the seal has decided to haul out, it hangs around just offshore, apparently testing the movement of the water column and waves before making its move. A seal uses its natural buoyancy and surfs landwards on a wave as it swashes up the shore, even when this is a steep rock ledge. Gripping the slippery seaweed and limpet-festooned rocks with its ten long and strong fore-claws, adding friction through maximum body surface contact with shore, the seal clings on as the backwash sucks down towards the sea. When the next wave hits, the seal is ready and reacts to its increased buoyancy by thrusting its whole body onwards and upwards in a cycle to be repeated until the seal is completely clear of the water. In this way, a seal navigates a situation where humans would be ripped to shreds! As seals forage underwater, all their available oxygen is prioritized for their diving activity. Oxygen is necessary for healthy digestion, so a seal

Seals high up on rocks above the sea

must wait until it returns to an oxygen-rich environment at the surface or at a haul-out to begin digesting its food. Seals may bottle (float vertically, head and nose visible at the sea surface, for an extended period without full submersion, resembling a floating bottle), or haul out every few days to rest and aid the digestion of their food. In addition, seals leave the sea more frequently and for longer periods during their annual moult (winter/spring) and breeding season (autumn/winter).

At the sea surface, a seal preparing to dive uses its muscles to open its nostrils to inhale and exhale a few times. Immediately prior to diving, the seal expels all air from its lungs and ducks its head lower than its tail, using its hindquarters to propel itself downwards. Breathing out before diving, and taking no air on dives, prevents a seal suffering from decompression sickness – or the bends – as a result of pressure changes when returning to the surface. On average, grey seals dive to

Female seal bananaing (above). Seal bottling and yawning (right)

around 70 m and for about 12 minutes. During this time, oxygen is stored in the haemoglobin and myoglobin in blood and muscles, which are tolerant to the build-up of lactic acid, and circulation is largely limited to a few vital organs – brain, heart and lungs. On deep dives, grey seals reduce their heart rate to just a few beats a minute; the longer the dive, the longer the seal must remain at the surface to repay its oxygen debt.

Seals' adaptations to the cold are more obvious. A blubber layer of 6–10 cm thick in adults provides insulation; two layers of dense fur help to reduce wind chill on land. Most heat is lost through the extremities – face and flippers – which have little blubber.

A dry, hauled-out seal splashed by a rising tide feels the cold water most at its extremities, which results in 'bananaing' – a characteristic behavioural reaction, where the seal lifts its head and tail in an arc at the same time! A seal's flippers possess counter-current heat exchange systems: veins wrap around arteries, recapturing warmth and returning it with blood back to the body. In contrast, seals hauled out in direct summer sunshine may overheat because of their effective insulation. At such times, seals may splay their webbing wide on both rear flippers, exposing them to the air and cold sand to maximize heat loss. Digging like a turtle on a beach to reach cooler sand may additionally aid heat loss.

Seal Senses

Seal head, showing ear, damp eye, eyebrows, whiskers and nose hairs

Grey seals are thought to navigate using a combination of senses. One of the most evocative features of a seal is its eyes – deep black pools that gaze at your soul! Large apertures capture more light in murky depths, but increase the possibilities of damage. Protection comes from regular secretions that cover the corneas. A healthy, well-hydrated seal 'cries' constant tears that form damp 'panda' patches around the eyes. Even blind seals have been known to survive in the wild, as their other senses compensate for the loss of sight. While a seal's eye is designed to see underwater, seals appear to be able to see movements even across great distances – for example, between themselves and a cliff top, so keeping out of sight while watching them, and maintaining a low profile on the skyline, are particularly important ways of reducing disturbance. Even though they have no external ears, seals have very sensitive hearing, particularly to high-pitched, loud or unusual sounds. Although complicated by ambient sound levels, wind direction, wind strength and echoes from rocky cliffs, seals have been known to hear an approaching engine before a human, and they are particularly attuned to changing noise levels. Sound appears to alert a seal to danger first.

Seal head, showing closed eyes while sleeping, whiskers and nose hairs

When feeding, particularly in waters with poor visibility, a seal's most important sense is probably feeling vibrational movement in the sea picked up by its whiskers, or vibrissae. A seal may be sensitive to the movement of fish several minutes ahead of it. As a seal dries out on land, its vibrissae curl gracefully at the ends. A seal has between three and six pairs of eyebrows; up to 50 pairs of whiskers, and two single hairs – rhinal vibrissae – on top and either side of its nose, presumably for fine-tuning directional vibrations.

Smell appears to play a significant role in a seal's life. A newly hauled-out seal greets other seals by sniffing their snouts and ears. A seal mother instantly recognizes the smell of her own pup, immediately recoiling from the scent of another pup approached in error.

Knowing What You're Looking At

A grey seal's coat of many colours

Contrary to the image conjured up by their name, grey seals exhibit a huge natural variation. Their colours range from black to white and cream to chocolate, with all combinations in between. Pale, plain-coloured seals are often wrongly described as pups, even when they are very large. Likewise, smallish honey- or ginger-coloured plain seals, but these are juveniles leading up to an elongated first annual moult. Seal fur is very soft, and replenished every year during the annual late winter and spring moult, after which seals look their most pristinely beautiful as they sport their brand new fur coats.

As a species, grey seals are sexually dimorphic, averaging 2.3 m long, with larger males up to 3 m long (the longest recorded by the Cornwall Wildlife Trust Marine Strandings Network was 2.8 m), and weighing in at 230–300 kg. Females are smaller – to up to 2 m long, weighing up to 180 kg.

The easiest way to work out the gender of a seal from a distance is to look at its belly!

A classically marked adult male seal (left), and a 'girly' young male (right)

A classically marked adult female seal (left), and a plain dark adult female (right)

All seals have an umbilicus mark and two nipples on the underside of their lower abdomen, but males have an additional aperture called a prepuce (sometimes highlighted by a linear worn patch from the prepuce down towards the rear flippers.) If the seal is un-co-operative and lying on its belly, then you are generally advised to look at the overall appearance of its fur or pelage pattern. On an imaginary pelage pattern spectrum from plain to spotty, adult male seals tend to be darker and plainer, while females tend to be lighter and spottier. This holds true for about 80 per cent of seals, but there are exceptions to confound us all!

A much better way of distinguishing male from female seals is to look at their heads (page 20). Male grey seals have far longer and broader snouts than females of the same age; females have much smaller heads with finer features – they are prettier! In addition, older males tend to get a more exaggerated convex nose profile than older females, and males develop a ruff of wrinkles around their thicker necks, as well as picking up numerous scars from sparring with each other.

As grey seals get older, they grow lengthways. They all begin life covered in long white fluffy fur called a lanugo, which is thought to have given them camouflage when they were born on winter snow and ice. Seals under three weeks of age have white coats, which begin to moult off at different rates for different pups – some are fully moulted into their adult pelage pattern at two weeks; others still have a few tufts of white fur left

Top: Heads of adult grey seals: male (left), and female (right)
Above: White-coated pup (left), and golden-brown juvenile (right)

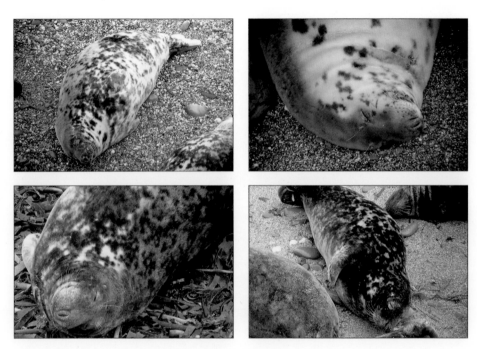

Four distinctive fur patterns, clockwise from top left: 'Black Rabbit', 'Parallels', 'Pacific' and 'Lost Boy'

at four weeks. Grey seals are described as juveniles up to the age of four years, having a thin, sleek appearance. At around four years old, many seals suddenly balloon outwards, becoming much fatter as they reach adulthood. They are hardest to age at this time. Large adult grey seals can only really be aged approximately from observation of their heads. Adult seals get a more convex nose profile with increasing age, and adult males get broader and longer snouts.

Each seal has a unique fur pattern, as distinctive as a fingerprint, from which it can be individually identified, and many hours can be spent inventing pictures from their fur patterns, in the way we see images in clouds

Seals moulting

and ink blots. Names are inspired by creative imaginations applied to a seal's fur patterns, made more challenging by the fact that different people 'see' different things there.

A seal's fur pattern remains for life, but the contrast within the pattern may change over time as the seal ages. The resolution of the fur pattern diminishes during the annual moult, as pigments in the old fur break down, turn-

ing the fur brown as it drops out, to reveal fresh 'high definition' black, grey and white fur patterns beneath. Likewise, patterns can be masked as a seal's love of rolling around on sandy beaches disguises its identity. Sleek, wet fur lies flush and smoothly against a seal's body, making fur patterns crystal clear as it emerges from the sea to haul on to land. Exposed to air, the fur begins to stand on end,

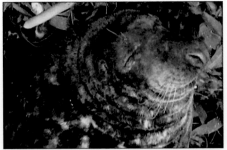

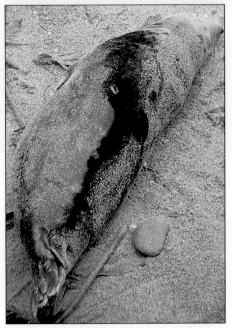

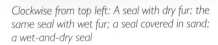

Clockwise from top left: A seal with dry fur; the same seal with wet fur; a seal covered in sand; a wet-and-dry seal

perpendicular to the skin as it dries, blurring patterns that seep into each other.

Photo-identification enables us to unobtrusively follow individual seals throughout their lives, both spatially and temporally, and this is beginning to reveal many secrets about the private lives of seals around our coast.

The Secret Lives of Grey Seals

Watching individual seals grow up is a real privilege; witnessing the key events in their lives is very special, and watching a new life begin is an awe-inspiring experience. A seal's calendar is different from ours, and seals seem to live through three main seasons a year. The first is key to their survival…

- *The breeding season*. This begins in September and continues until December, although white-coated seal pups have been observed in every month of the year in Cornwall.
- *The moulting season*. From January to May, seals are at their most grumpy and craggy, as they lose and replace all their fur.
- *The offshore foraging season*. Seals feed all year round, but their main time for focusing on food and fattening up is between June and August. At this time, the mainland haul-out beaches are abandoned in favour of more remote offshore haul-outs, which presumably become popular because they are closer to rich foraging grounds.

The breeding season

One unspectacular late September morning, Simon and I were lying on a cliff edge peering at the reasonable-sized haul-out of seals beneath us. With around 40 seals, there was plenty of activity to keep us entertained. Beachmaster 'W' was calmly in control, keeping the testosterone levels of the other wannabe beachmasters, 'S Hook' and 'Feathers', at bay. We had felt honoured to watch mother 'Walking Fingers' feed her pup 'Treasure', and all was well with the world. As I routinely scanned my binoculars across the beach, I noticed something unusual out of the corner of one eye. One of the seals was quivering in a strange fashion. Seals often shiver as they emerge from the sea, but this wasn't really a shiver, just more of a quiver! We had already talked about the seal in question, as she was an unusually dark female, being milk-chocolate coloured all over with just a few white markings, and she was heavily pregnant – very, very heavily pregnant. Seals are generally fattest around their waists, but pregnant females are usually obvious, being

'Kelp', clockwise from top left: being born; shortly after birth; an hour old; being fed at three days old. Bottom right: two mothers with their pups

fattest around their lower abdomen and carrying a lot of excess blubber all over. We had a brief conversation about moving around the cliff top to get a closer look, but feared we might miss something in the short time this would take, and were distracted by another cliff-top onlooker, whose barking dog scared a lot of the

The bond between pup and mother is strong (left).
The mother's milk is 50 per cent fat (above)

*seals into the sea. Cursing, we looked back at
the quivering seal, who despite being nearest to
the disturbance was one of the only seals not
to have shifted by even a centimetre. At that
moment, her contractions began – about three
sets of four big contractions. As we watched,
a small white 'tennis ball' emerged between
her rear flippers, and expanded to the size
of a football, before being suddenly sucked
back in. The mother seal looked surprised and*

*turned her head to look for a pup, but none was
there, so she settled for the next contractions.
One more set and the football returned, the
pup emerging head first (though they are so
streamlined, with no long appendages, that the
pups can be born either way round) and, as its
rear flippers flopped out and somersaulted over
its head, the umbilicus twanged, and the pup,
still in its intact sac, was lying prone and still
on the beach. A few nerve-racking milliseconds*

passed before the pup suddenly twitched, stretching its neck forwards and splitting the sac over the top of its unsteady head. What a shock it must be to leave a wonderfully warm, dark space for a cold, hard beach on a bright September day! A series of sneezes helped the pup 'Kelp' to clear its passages and take its first breath of life. We were speechless.

The next few hours would be critical to Kelp's wellbeing. Pups seem to be born on outgoing tides, giving them a precious 12 hours to acclimatize to their surroundings. Nourished immediately prior to birth, Kelp was not hungry and didn't want feeding. First feeds are notoriously anxious times, and Kelp's instinct drew him to his mother a few hours later; yet his lack of previous experience of suckling left him at a loss as to what to do. Kelp's mother carefully manoeuvred to place her body in exactly the right spot for Kelp to suckle, but he was more interested in following the stronger scent of her flippers and head, leading him to move in entirely the wrong direction. All this made for 30 minutes of very painful viewing… 'Will he? … Won't he?', with everything depending on Kelp's ability to find the life-saving, nutrient-rich, over 50 per cent fat, first milk from his mother that would protect him with natural immunity. After many near misses, Kelp finally latched on to first one and then the other of his mother's teats, and it was almost as if he expanded in size as his rolls of skin filled with the volume of milk he consumed. Audible gasps were heard from the cliff top as we remembered to breathe again.

Most new-born pups weigh in at around 13–14 kg, and are about a metre-long mass of skin and bone. Rolls of skin give a misleading impression of health, but they are ready for the exponential growth that a pup will make in its first three weeks of life. Pups that are a few days old have a clear umbilicus of varying length that will change from bright pink to black before falling off. Pups look their most photogenic up to three days old, but they are very vulnerable. Should high tides and big swells drag them seawards, they would struggle to survive, whereas pups over three days old can cope with swimming in all but the worst sea conditions, under their mother's attentive supervision. The bond between mother and pup is very strong, and a mother can instantly tell her pup with a call or a sniff. Pups feed a little and often to begin with, averaging once every four hours for a few minutes, and for longer periods, less frequently – every seven or so hours – as they near weaning at 15–21 days. By the end of the second week, they look like fat torpedos, and after three weeks they resemble barrels

'Missee', a day-old pup, with her exhausted mother

– so fat, they must dig a hole in the sand to rest their heads. At around 40 kg they are weaned, and without any demonstrations from mother, hunger guides them to the sea, where they must head out into the harsh world of the open ocean and teach themselves to feed.

The mother, however, is left exhausted from rearing her pup. Having remained close to it, on the beach, in the sea cave or keeping a line of sight to her pup from the sea for three weeks, she has been prevented from proactive feeding. As her pup has put on 30+ kg, so the mother has lost a third

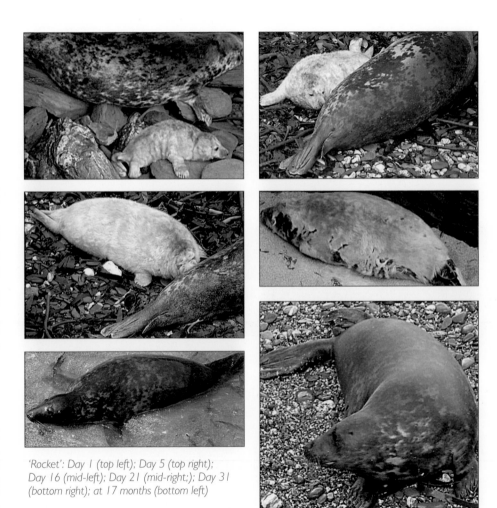

'Rocket': Day 1 (top left); Day 5 (top right);
Day 16 (mid-left); Day 21 (mid-right;); Day 31
(bottom right); at 17 months (bottom left)

In three weeks, 'Storm' grows as his mother shrinks

on land or in the sea. Having aggressively resisted the beachmaster's advances for around three weeks, the female finally accepts his approach at about the time her pup is weaned. Lying with his belly to her back, the business of mating appears to take place quickly. Thereafter, the two seals lie together quietly for a while. One mating pair observed at sea lay intertwined and motionless, floating at the surface for over 20 minutes. As they occasionally rolled over, the female sculled with her fore-flippers to enable them both to breathe restfully at the surface. Seals appear their most serene at this time. Unable to sustain a pregnancy in her worn-out state, the female's fertilized egg divides a few times, before becoming dormant in a process called delayed implantation. If, over the next three months, she feeds well, regaining her health and strength, the blastocyst implants in the womb lining and develops normally – her pregnancy begins again. In effect, seal mothers can be pregnant for 12 months of the year, every year for their entire lives! In practice, in some years, females are unable to regain their weight and health fast enough after suckling their pup, so the fertilized egg doesn't implant and the pregnancy ends. However, some females can and do have pups annually. With a gestation period of around eight

of her body weight and, with protruding hip bones, looks totally emaciated. Yet at this time she is at her most attractive to the dominant 'beachmaster' seal who mates with her months from implantation, seal mothers tend to give birth to their pups at roughly the same time every year, and at a similar location.

One adult female seal, 'Ghost' (photo page 26, right), is our most special mother. Appearing with her first pup, which she successfully weaned, on 3 November, Ghost delighted us by returning every year to the same beach to give birth to new pups on 21 October the next year, and on 17 October, 16 October, 8 October, 15 October and 9 October in consecutive years. Sadly, her sixth pup, 'Shadow', was one of three pups to die on the same night in very high spring tides in stormy seas, but as grey seal pup mortality rates are 40–60 per cent in the first year of life, Ghost has done brilliantly to successfully raise six out of seven pups in as many years.

After seal pups leave the beach of their birth, their natal site, they are thought to explore their new underwater world, during a period referred to as a post-weaning dispersal. Inept feeders to begin with, young pups eat anything and lose a lot of weight before gaining some as they become more competent hunters. A year-old seal is only distinguishable from a recently weaned pup in its length, as it is unlikely to be much fatter.

Female seals: juvenile (top); mature adult (above)

Seal pups are thought to make mental maps of the marine world they visit, and some pups swim hundreds of kilometres in their first year. One seal pup, satellite-tagged by the Sea Mammal Research Unit in north Wales, swam to Rosslare in south-east Ireland, the Isles of Scilly, and visited a few kilometres off the Brittany coast before returning to the south coast of Cornwall – a journey

Two wet juveniles playing on the beach, about to wake up a dry 'White ring teddy stripe'!

of around 1,000 kilometres – at the ripe old age of three months. In Cornwall, so far, just two pups have been observed to return to their natal site, and both 17 months after they left. These two special seals are 'Curly' and 'Rocket'. Curly's return is particularly sig-

nificant, as being female, it will be interesting to see if she chooses to have her pups in the area where she was born. But we must wait at least seven years to find out.

The juvenile years of a seal appear relaxed and anxiety free. Naturally playful, young

Juveniles playing in shallow water

seals are frequently observed interacting with each other, and generally disturbing the older adult seals which prefer to sleep on the haul-out beach.

Seals' greeting sniffs appear to inform them about friends and foes. Friends may be seen in pairs or small groups, rolling around at the water's edge, especially during the breeding season, practising the moves they will need as adults. Foes may trigger flight responses, as seals rapidly haul away, splashing into the shallows and doing a beach-start from 0 to

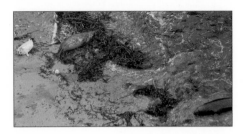

Mother 'Walking Fingers'; father 'W', and pup 'Treasure'

60 in no time, as rear flippers thrash from side to side, propelling the seal into the safety of deeper water. Much of this play is mischievous, and involves a lot of body contact.

Most adult male seals barely register it is the breeding season. Each seal-breeding location has a dominant male, referred to as the 'beachmaster'. Strong leadership from the beachmaster results in a calm haul-out, where all the seals respect the boss. Insecure leaders with poor leadership skills may result in anxiety-ridden haul-outs, frequently disturbed by marauding wannabe males challenging the beachmaster in fearsome fights, albeit short in duration. Sleeping seals are forced to scatter as sparring males move obliviously around the haul-out, disturbing the rest. Females always protest, and adult females appear to be the only seals capable of dominating the beachmasters. As a

female's personal space is invaded, she invariably howls a loud warning at the interloper, signalling him to leave. If he doesn't leave her alone, she continues howling, using her fore-flippers to repeatedly swat him, and lunging her neck forward to snap at him. Most beachmasters understand this message, and communicate their lack of threat and subservience to her by slowing rolling away from her, before backing off to leave the female to sleep soundly. Only a few adult males get to be beachmaster, winning them the chance to pass on their genes to future generations. The strongest of beachmasters dominate a haul-out for several years, fathering most of the pups from that location. As a result of a year separating mating and birth, and the difficulties of spotting pups at breeding locations, only one incidence has been recorded so far of a mother, father and pup being on the beach together at one time.

The moulting season

Early spring sees the largest haul-outs of seals on mainland sites, with seals spending less time at sea. Females moult before males, but there is an overlap, and huge numbers

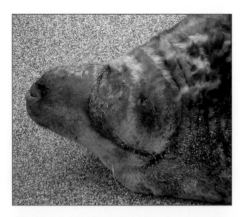

Moulting seal with blood transfer around the eye

so close to the surface of their skin, seals are particularly vulnerable at this time. While losing heat, energy can be conserved by hauling out and sleeping. Human disturbance during the moulting season can be particularly expensive to a seal's energy budget, compromising the seal's nutritional state for the rest of the year.

The offshore foraging season

of scruffy-looking seals litter our shores at this time of year (photos page 22). As the pigments in their old fur break down, pelages take on a browner appearance. Blood vessels near the skin surface open their widest to fuel the growth of new fur beneath the old. For whatever reason, this is when seals are at their most irritable and tetchy with each other. Frequent scratching with long, sharp fore-claws often results in broken and bleeding skin at this time of year. Re-scratched, the blood transfers to the flippers, and into arc-shaped lines on other areas of the seal's body as blood is again transferred during scratching. A seal with a superficial wound begins to look like a horror-movie victim! With blood

As summer approaches, seals begin to leave their mainland haul-out sites, favouring the many more remote offshore rocky islands around the Cornish coast. These sites are only easily accessed in calmer conditions, and specific haul-out locations vary according to the position of haul-out ramps at the particular time and tidal state at which the seal chooses to haul out. Often limited by the amount of haul-out space available, seal congregations tend to be smaller. Seals are thought to spend one in every four or five days hauled out to rest and digest the food caught in offshore foraging trips. Seals may travel from one haul-out to the next, covering long distances around the coast, or use a

'Woody' in north Cornwall (left), and off Lundy (right), showing ID tag circled in yellow

single haul-out as a base for all their foraging trips. This is the hardest time of year to keep tabs on the seals, and least is known about where they go, although we do get occasional insights.

'Woody' is a juvenile male seal, who needed to be rescued from Sennen as a fully moulted weaner at a couple of months old. Rehabilitated by the marvellous animal-care team at the National Seal Sanctuary at Gweek, Woody made good progress, being released four months later near Portreath. Within a month, Woody had been spotted by Cornwall Seal Group, thriving back in the wild, where he has been observed regularly ever since. At the age of three years, Woody was recorded as 'going on his holidays'. In late April, he was identified at a north-coast haul-out in west Cornwall. By early June, he was photographed by Bex Allen as he swam west of Newquay, and by the end of June, Woody was captured on an underwater camera by Keith Hiscock off the south-east coast of Lundy. By the end of August, Woody's foraging trip was over, and he was seen back where he started.

Little is known about the complexity of individual seal visits to particular seal sites, but seals appear to have seasonal visit patterns. Some seals visit a site only during the offshore foraging season, others only during the moulting season, and others only during the breeding season. Some seals stay for two of the three seal seasons, and a few may remain all year round, as shown in the charts.

(A)

(A)	2	3	4	5	6	7	8	9	10
Jan									
Feb									
Mar									
Apr									
May		1			1		1	1	
Jun	2				1		2	1	
Jul	2	1					1	4	2
Aug	3	3	1	2	3	1	3	2	2
Sep	3		1	1	2	3	1	1	
Oct									1
Nov									
Dec	1	1							

(B)

(B)	3	4	5	6	7	8	9	10	11
Jan									
Feb				1					
Mar		2	1		2	1			1
Apr	1				1		1		
May									
Jun						1			
Jul						1			
Aug									
Sep									
Oct									
Nov									
Dec									

(C)

(C)	1	2	3	4	5	6	7	8
Jan		1						
Feb								
Mar								
Apr								
May								
Jun								
Jul								
Aug				1				
Sep								1
Oct	1	4	1	1	1		2	1
Nov		1		3				
Dec		1						

(D)

(D)	2	3	4	5	6	7	8	9	10
Jan						1	3	1	
Feb		1		1					1
Mar						3			1
Apr									1
May									
Jun									
Jul									
Aug									
Sep					1				
Oct	3		3	5	3	5	4	1	
Nov	1		5	4			1		
Dec			2	1	1	1			

Seal visits: (A) Mostly offshore foraging season; (B) Mostly moulting season; (C) Mostly breeding season; (D) Mostly breeding and moulting season. (Years across the top; numbers show identifications per month)

(E)

(E)	3	4	5	6	7	8	9	10
Jan			1			2		
Feb				1	1		2	
Mar			2	2	3			1
Apr			4	2	1	1		2
May		2	1		3			
Jun	2	1		2	2	1	1	
Jul	2			1	2	2	1	
Aug	2	1			1		1	
Sep	3							
Oct								
Nov								
Dec								

(F)

(F)	3	4	5	6	7	8	9	10
Jan								
Feb								1
Mar					1			1
Apr								
May				2		1		
Jun							1	
Jul	2	1	1		1	1		
Aug	2	1		1	2	2	1	3
Sep	3	1	1	3	2			1
Oct	1	2					2	2
Nov							1	1
Dec								

(G)

(G)	1	2	3	4	5	6	7	8	9	10
Jan		2			2		1	2		
Feb					2					
Mar					2	2	2	1		1
Apr					4	5	1	3	1	1
May			1		2	3	1	2	1	1
Jun	1			1		3			1	
Jul			1							1
Aug			1		5	2		3	1	2
Sep	1				3	4	6	2	2	2
Oct				3	7	9	4	1		1
Nov				4	3	2	2	1		2
Dec	1			3	1	5	1			1

Seal visits: (E) Mostly moulting and offshore foraging seasons; (F) Mostly offshore foraging and breeding seasons; (G) All seal seasons. (Years across the top; numbers show identifications per month)

'Zigzag': females are worth fighting over

Seal visit-patterns are made all the more complex as the patterns change with the life-cycle stage of each seal. So, for example, one juvenile female seal, 'Zigzag', visited a haul-out site for four years only during the foraging season; but as she matured to breeding age, her visit-pattern changed completely, and she then visited only during the moulting and breeding seasons and was absent during the foraging season. For three years, a juvenile male seal, 'Flying Bird', visited the haul-out only during the moulting and breeding seasons, before changing his visits gradually over another three years as he became a mature adult, to visiting just during the moulting season for a couple of years. The consistency of seasonal seal visits over several years may suggest that seals in Cornwall do have regular seasonal migration routes that they follow according to their life-cycle stage.

Thinking Like a Seal… at Work, Rest and Play

Favourite seal places

As a human, it is hard to assess what makes a good seal haul-out site. To try to really understand what a seal is up to, you have to think like a seal. Top priority for a seal must be food, followed by rest, as this is essential for effective digestion. Grey seals are very social creatures, and they appear to seek out the company of other seals for at least part of the year. As juveniles, interaction is expressed through active play, where seals of both sexes practise the moves they will need for survival into adulthood. As adults, company is sought to provide added security as they sleep, and for most females and some males, to mate.

Understanding some of a seal's basic needs gives us an insight into the kinds of habitats grey seals must make use of. To complete their life-cycle, grey seals around the coast of Cornwall need at least four main kinds of habitat:

- *Breeding habitat*. In Cornwall, seal pups are born in sea caves, or in remote coves made up of sand and shingle, or boulder-beaches, or both. Breeding females and males show breeding-site fidelity, returning to the same sites during the breeding season year after year until, as a female, they are too old to sustain a pregnancy, or, as a male, they get ousted by a bigger and stronger beachmaster. The best, most established, breeding areas must be passed down through generations, but new and more marginal areas may be used if the main site is full to capacity. Recently, a popular open-beach breeding spot was taken out of action by a major rockfall, blocking access to the seals' favourite alcove under the cliff, and completely changing the morphology of the shore. What had been a gently sloping, sandy area became a steep boulder-slope of sharp-edged, unweathered rocks. It had been a great relief that the rockfall had taken place before the breeding season, albeit only by a week:

Breeding caves (left). Breeding habitat: boulder beach (right). Spot the seal!

any later, mothers and pups would almost certainly have been crushed to death. As the breeding season developed, the alterations made by the rockfall caused mayhem with the mothers and their pups, as they could no longer access areas above high tide, and in big seas at least two mothers had to escort their pups around to the adjacent cove and out of sight, to a new area which then became overcrowded. While we were unable to see the results, the echoing howls of mothers getting in each other's way could frequently be heard from the cliff tops, along with the higher-pitched calls of their hungry pups. Most breeding sites are only used during the breeding season, and are strangely devoid of any seal activity during the rest of the year. A few breeding sites – probably the more marginal ones – may also function as haul-out habitat.

- *Haul-out habitat.* This is where seals are most vulnerable to human disturbance. There are two kinds of seal haul-out sites: *(a) Onshore:* These sites are mostly and almost exclusively used during the breeding and moulting seasons, and it is here that the largest gatherings of seals can be seen. *(b) Offshore:* Gently sloping rocky ledges around offshore islands, generally used more during the offshore foraging season. Optimal haul-out habitat is hard to pin down, with many sites that look ideal, even those adjacent to established sites,

Onshore haul-out habitats (above and left)

remaining unused. Key features probably include more than one access route, so if danger enters via one entrance, the seals can leave through another exit. Entrances must be easily accessible for seals, so sites must have suitable haul-out ramps at a variety of tidal heights. Protection from the worst of the rough seas is also desirable. Rock skerries, or reefs just out to sea, help to break up the worst of the waves, giv-

Offshore haul-out habitats

ing more shelter to the haul-out site. More exposed offshore islands need suitable leeward sides with protective morphology. Finally, an ability to get out of the prevailing wind reduces the effect of wind chill. These factors combined to explain why the two main onshore seal haul-out sites are located on the north Cornish coast, with only small seal haul-outs occurring on the south coast. Seals are intelligent, and seek out the most sheltered locations, according to human activity and the prevailing conditions, which is most obvious in the Isles of Scilly.

- *Foraging habitat.* Least is known about this aspect of grey-seal habitat, although ideas can be gathered from what is known about seal diet and diving behaviour. Grey seals are opportunistic bottom-feeders, and are thought to nuzzle around the seabed, searching with their whiskers and aiming to disturb sand eels, snapping them up as they emerge from the sand. Sand eels are the preferred food of grey seals, and make up the bulk of their diet, although seals feed on a wide variety of fish species, particularly benthic (bottom-dwelling) species and gadoids (soft-finned fish). Foraging habitat must therefore be linked to large areas of sand and gravel substrates, that favour sand-eel grounds. Knowing that seals dive on average to 70 m also begins to delimit seal-foraging sites.

- *Transit habitat.* As seals move around the Cornish coast, and beyond to the Celtic fringe, they need transit routes linking

Foraging habitats: offshore (above); onshore (left)

all the other three types of seal habitat. Whether these transit routes are narrow seal motorways linking haul-out service stations, or are generalized 'freedom to roam' areas of sea is something we have yet to discover.

Understanding the key elements of grey-seal habitat and how they interface with seal seasons is essential for the effective future con-

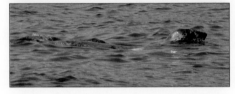

Seals swimming in the sea

servation of the species. Interestingly, many areas of coast favoured by seals across Cornwall and the rest of England are owned by the National Trust, in whose care seals thrive.

Varied behaviours

A quick glance at a seal haul-out site may give the impression of passive inactivity, with most seals sleeping soundly. Careful observation over even a short time can reveal a wide range of varied, often amusing behaviours,

and detailed knowledge of individual seals often exposes the fluid nature of a haul-out, as seals that one minute are sleeping may have a quick scrap and then disappear into the sea, only to return a few minutes later, wander around the haul-out, annoying other seals, before finding the perfect spot and falling asleep again. Take your eye off a seal haul-out and, within minutes, it is all change – like only opening your eyes when the participants are sat down during a game of musical chairs!

Behaviours are best categorized according to where the seals are – in the sea, on land, or moving between the two.

From top: Bottling, diving, snorkelling

Sea-based behaviours

- *Swimming:* Seals move gracefully through the water, propelled by sideways movements of alternately fanned rear flippers. Over long distances, seals swim at an average speed of 4 km an hour, covering around 100 km a day. Seals can, of course, swim much faster than this, and from a still beach-start, a seal can attain a very fast speed in just a few seconds.

- *Bottling:* Sleeping vertically in the sea, its nose poking through the surface, a seal may resemble a floating bottle. Seals breathe erratically, opening their nostrils a few times and then holding their breath. They may sink vertically during their sleep, and when carbon dioxide levels rise in their blood, a reflex in their rear flippers causes a twitch that returns them to the surface. Seals may bottle in the same location for some time, or may intersperse bottling with diving cycles, when they have been observed to sleep in a chosen place on the seabed.

- *Logging:* Alternatively, seals may sleep horizontally at the surface of the sea. This can be one of the most worrying behaviours to watch, as such seals appear to be dead, only giving themselves away when they scull with their flippers, or very slightly raise their nostrils clear of the water to breath.

- *Eating:* Surprisingly, this is a relatively rare sight. A hungry seal gulps down a fish in one, and only if the fish is too big will the seal bring it to the surface. The central part of the fish may be held in the mouth as the seal shakes its head violently to break the fish apart. The seal will allow broken chunks of fish to sink, and then dives down to retrieve them in turn. Alternatively, the seal may hold the fish in its fore-flippers as it treads water at the surface, biting chunks out of the fish; but a seal's fore-flipper digits are not very dexterous, so they don't make great fish clamps.

- *Diving:* Seals usually dive head first, having expelled all the air from their lungs, using their rear flippers to power them downwards. It is always amusing to see whitecoat pups trying to dive against their natural buoyancy, which usually leaves their rear flippers splashing about at the surface, until their lower abdominal muscles grow strong enough to develop more propulsion to counteract their buoyancy. One-week old pups have been seen successfully diving underwater, but they soon 'boing' back up to the surface! Young seals have been seen to go underwater and then let out bubbles of air which rise and burst at the surface, breaking in big rings that ripple out concentrically, confusing any onlooker who turned too late to see the seal. In such cases, the seal must have premeditated the action, by holding a small amount of air in its mouth, which it later released underwater.

- *Snorkelling:* Seals that are relaxed and resting at the surface may position their nostrils half in and half out of the water. As air is exhaled from their lungs explosively, it creates bubbles that accompany the seal's audible snorts. Occasionally, seals may be heard before they are seen, and may be given away by their loud snorting, but this tends to be an adult behaviour.

Some offshore water-based behaviours are more social, and involve more than one seal:

- *Dancing:* This graceful and acrobatic behaviour is a real treat to watch. Two or more seals swim around each other, sometimes in spirals in very close proximity. Occasionally, seals are seen performing synchronized swimming movements worth a 9.5 on anyone's scoring system!

- *Splashing:* Using a fore-flipper to create a splash at the surface is common attention-seeking behaviour. In contrast, seals may also splash to deter unwanted attention,

Dancing at the water's edge (left). Crash-diving due to disturbance (bottom left of photo, right)

when another seal is too close to them in the water. Interestingly, this behaviour is sometimes used to gain human attention, particularly in harbours where seals beg for food. Please always resist the temptation to feed wild seals as, for reasons explained on page 72 – doing so has damaging impacts on both seals and humans.

- *Fighting:* Aggressive fights are rare, and usually only occur during the breeding season. A particularly fierce one that took place off a key breeding site involved a lot of loud snarling and splashing. It was difficult to see precisely what was going on, but the seals were aiming to bite their opponent's neck, and once gripped shook their heads as roughly as possible. In Cornwall, fights

don't often last long, as it soon becomes clear which is the strongest, bravest seal, and the pretender gives in quickly. The funniest aspect of these serious contests is the effect they have on other seals hauled out in the area, which react like children in a school playground, all rushing to gather around the fight. In this way, perhaps, a beachmaster's reputation is strengthened, as some younger males will not bother to challenge the beachmaster, having witnessed how he dealt with bigger and stronger seals!

- *Crash-diving:* Seals that are spooked and scared at sea by something or someone crash-dive very suddenly, causing a great splash visually and audibly. This instant reaction is followed by the uncertain seal returning to the surface a short distance away to take another look at what spooked it. If it remains scared, it may crash-dive again, or react with curiosity, exploring the stimulus instead.

- *Tracking:* People at sea in slow-moving, human-powered vessels, are a constant source of amusement to seals. Although often wary of silent craft that sneak up on them at water level, seals may choose to observe this potential threat from a safe distance, and usually from behind. So effectively a seal tracks the vessel, looking at it for a few seconds and then swimming underwater to keep up with it. As seals often snort just before they dive, the vessel's puzzled occupants look around. It is almost as if the seal waits until they have looked away again before returning to the surface for another good look.

Land-based behaviours

- *Sleeping:* Seals sleep in a variety of positions on the beach. Many just lie on their bellies, falling asleep the moment their head touches the sand, although they remain vigilant, looking up regularly; vigilance becomes less active as they settle down and are reassured about their safety. Other

Seals sleeping (top); pillow-talk (above)

seals prefer to sleep on their sides, and some may have a preferred side to sleep on. Very relaxed seals, which have been out of the sea for a longer period of time, lie on their backs, exposing their bellies and curling their rear flippers around each other in a cute fashion.

Stretching (above left); yawning (above right), and head-rubbing (left)

pers. Yawns tend to be great gaping affairs, accompanied by the head rolling back and around in a circle, which exaggerates the usually silent yawn. A yawn is often followed by open-mouthed tongue licks.

- *Head-rubbing:* This activity often accompanies yawning. A seal uses a partly fanned-out fore-flipper to wipe over the top or side of its head and face, in an action that appears to give it great satisfaction.

- *Hauling:* The hauling action of seals has been described (pages 12–13), but it is worth noting that, over soft substrates, seals leave distinctive haul trails. A single drag-line, slightly narrower than the seal's

- *Stretching and yawning:* Sleep is regularly broken up with rear-flipper fanning and whole-body stretches, showing how flexible seals are. A seal can arc its body so far that its nose touches its rear flip-

Seal on the move (above left). Haul trail of pup (above right). Scratching breakdance (right)

body, has paired fore-flipper prints either side of it, sometimes with sand thrown up in front of the print in the same direction as the seal was moving. The speed at which the seal was moving corresponds to the distance between these prints. Prints close together are made by a relaxed, slow-moving seal, whereas prints far apart tell you the seal was moving at speed. One of the few times a seal's tail is held straight upwards is when it is hauling over shingle or boulders.

- *Scratching:* This is a common activity for hauled-out seals, particularly during the moulting season when seals seem to be at their most sensitive. As with humans, most itches are accessible, the ones on

their backs posing the greatest challenge. An irresistible back itch that just has to be scratched results in the most amusing of all seal behaviours – the breakdance! The seal is forced to writhe in three dimensions,

Sand-snuffling (left). Big strong alpha male (right)

which often results in it moving sideways across the beach.

- *Bananaing:* This behaviour has already been described (page 15). It is the reaction of a dry seal to being showered or washed over by the surf, often on a rising tide. As seals tend to prefer lying close to the edge of the sea, their position must change as the tide goes out and comes in. As a result, it is not unusual for groups of seals to be seen bananaing together. The banana behaviour continues with each incoming wave, until the seal finally decides either to go into the sea, or to move further up the beach, where the behaviour will have to be repeated a short while later. Should the

seal decide to return to the sea, it will tolerate its body being covered in water, followed by its rear flippers, but sometimes a seal is seen swimming out to sea with a completely dry head above the water, as if it simply can't bear the cold and will only dive at the last possible minute

- *Digging and sand-snuffling:* This is one of the rarer seal behaviours. Seals have been seen using their snouts to dig down or snuffle into the sand, apparently following a scent – possibly of a previous seal – or the behaviour may be linked to feeding actions on the seabed. Sometimes the seal progresses to digging with its fore-flippers alternately, in an action resembling a turtle.

Some land-based behaviours are more social and involve more than one seal:

- *Prone howling:* This is a behaviour that appears to be limited to juvenile males as they become adults. Apparently wild with rampaging hormones, these poor young males give the impression of being in unbearable pain. Their howling is often the first aspect of this behaviour to be noticed. The afflicted youngster rolls around the beach, stretching his body lengthways until he resembles a thin sausage. He then extends his telescopic neck and presses it down on to the sand before emitting long, slow piercing howls. While this whole melodrama looks very worrying and may last a considerable time, the perpetrator usually stops quite suddenly, resuming normal service as if nothing had happened.

- *Body-slapping:* Often in conjunction with prone howling, a few juvenile males have been observed deliberately lifting up their bodies from wet sand and slamming them back down, in order to make a loud slapping noise accompanied by a big splash. This behaviour is thought to be attention-seeking, as if to say, 'Look at me! I'm a big, strong seal!' Body-slapping may be repeated a few times, followed by a bit of threatening behaviour.

Lucky male sniff-greeted by two females

- *Princess behaviour – the tart!:* Young females coming into season for the first time spend a lot of time trying to attract male attention. They pester sleeping males, repeatedly approaching and sniffing them, howling and flippering at them if they get no reaction. When the sleepy males finally wake and take an interest, the princess shoots down to the water provocatively, returning to irritate the males if they need reminding of the female presence. In extreme cases, young females shake their head wildly from side to side, and rush around the beach in a crazy fashion.

'Spade', a young female seal, was showing off to a group of males that were studiously ignor-

From top: Sniff greeting

ing her. Unbeknown to Spade, she had gained the attention of 'Teddy', a very large old male further along the beach. Teddy dragged himself out of his slumber, and hauled across to where Spade was tormenting the group of younger males. He approached cautiously, and began sniffing her. Spade looked horrified at the appearance of her new suitor, and seemed to shrink in size before our very eyes, apparently hoping for a hole in the sand to swallow her up. She tried to escape, but Teddy followed on behind. Fortunately, Teddy was a wise old seal, and somewhat of a gentleman! He soon returned to his slumber, leaving Spade a little shaken, and hopefully a little less wanton!

• *Sniffing:* All seals greet each other with a sniff, first of the nose or mouth and sometimes around the ear hole; the behaviour is usually reciprocated by the other seal. Sometimes a seal sniffs and hardly causes a reaction, then both seals will settle down or move on. Other times, a recoil reaction is observed, perhaps as the seals fail to recognize one another, or recognize each other as a foe. One seal may then leave, or both may growl or snarl, perhaps even fight or chase each other down the beach and into the sea. Rocket's mother (page 29), who was blind in one eye, once approached the wrong pup, as she returned from the sea to feed him. Her first sniff of the pup resulted in a recoil action, and she hurriedly turned and moved away in search of Rocket. Abandoned pups often approach other seals on the beach, searching for their mother and a feed. Females turning around to sniff them often appear to dislike the smell, and retreat from the pup.

- *Flippering:* Seals usually like to have their own personal space, only occasionally tolerating ongoing physical contact with other seals. Adult females can be particularly vociferous about this, and howl toward the invader of their personal space. If this doesn't work, they turn around and swat the offending seal repeatedly with a fore-flipper. Occasionally, this doesn't work either, and then, interestingly and somewhat surprisingly, both seals may just go to sleep, in close proximity or touching each other.

- *Playing:* Young seals seem to love playing, and do so for hours on end. Two or more of them roll around each other in the shallows, or chase each other across the beach, waking up all the adults in an annoying fashion. Photo-identification shows that

Seals playing

two seals may end up playing around for days on end, either with the same seal or with a different partner. Sometimes playing groups are all male, or male and female, but it is quite unusual to see two young females playing together. Occasionally, the adults object to being woken, and split up the playing juveniles; but once the air is clear and it has all calmed down, the playing individuals often reunite and resume their games.

- *Rolling-pinning:* A particularly popular playing manoeuvre for juvenile seals is the 'rolling pin'. Here one seal positions itself at right angles mid-way to its partner's back before launching itself over the top of its

Rolling-pinning

partner and pinning the partner to the sand. Once their fore-flippers are splayed wide across the partner's back for balance, the pinned seal can be rolled back and forth in play.

• *Chasing:* Seals of all ages may chase each other around the beach for numerous reasons, ranging from fun through to aggression. Seals that move very quickly across the beach are fun to watch; youngsters

Threatening behaviour (left). Males sparring (right)

may give the impression of bouncing along, due to the favourable power-to-weight ratios; older seals lumber at best.

- *Rolling:* This is a highly submissive behaviour, most frequently used by dominant adult males to show they are not a threat. Beachmasters regularly check out the females on their patch, sniffing them, presumably to see if they are ready to mate. Once a female makes it clear she is not ready to mate, by howling and flippering him, the beachmaster retreats, beginning with a roll or two to get away from her.
- *Threatening:* It is easy to tell when a seal is being threatening. Its open-mouthed stance, baring a full set of visibly sharp, interlocking teeth and the deep, snarling growls of males, or the higher-pitched howls of females, are unmistakeable. A rule of thumb for people working in seal rehabilitation centres is not to go within a broom handle's length of a seal unless treating it. The reason for this is that seals have elastic, telescopic necks that can lunge and instantaneously stretch to the length of a broom handle to bite you! The same is true on the beach, with seals lunging at each other to force the other to retreat. It is not uncommon for wild seals to end up with arc-shaped bite marks.
- *Fighting:* Fighting is clearly much more serious and aggressive than threatening, and involves more physical contact. Juvenile seals play-fight, and adult females strongly threaten to protect their pups; only adult males fight. Aggressors aim to move to lie next to each other side by side, in order to gain ground to lunge at, bite and grip their opponent's neck. Bites during fighting pull

Beachmaster fighting a challenger

the skin away from the blubber layer, and may result in chunks of flesh being ripped out, so a fight can be a bloody affair. Fighting males seem oblivious to everything around them, causing other seals to scatter, or injuring innocent bystanders. When a beachmaster is a strong leader, fighting is rare – often a look from the beachmaster is enough to scare all but the most evenly matched seals off his patch. Even well-matched males rarely fight for long, one soon realizing that discretion is the better part of valour.

- *Stampeding:* In a relaxed haul-out, seals lie facing in all directions, randomly across the beach. A haul-out that has been recently disturbed is characterized by seals all lining up to face the sea. Stampedes are always shocking as they begin so suddenly. Just one scared seal can trigger a stampede: as it bolts towards the sea, it sets up a domino reaction throughout the haul-out, and in no time all the seals are heading seawards. Stampedes are often quite loud, as pebbles and rocks are moved by the rushing seals. If the wind is blowing towards you, a stampede can be smelt too. Seals have a very sour, musky smell, and their rapid movement releases odours that carry in the wind.

Transitional behaviours

- *Emerging from the sea:* A seal arriving at a haul-out often practises a ritualistic routine of behaviour. As it enters the shallows to a beach, or the white water around an island, it looks vigilantly at the haul-out to search for the presence of other seals, and to get a feel for the movement of the water in the area. If other seals are present and the situation safe, the seal begins to emerge from the sea. Once clear of the water, it sometimes shakes its head, spraying water everywhere – presumably to clear its ears of water and then look around warily. Active nostrils reveal the seal to be sniffing the air carefully too, aiming to sense danger. If unsure, the seal may return to the sea, only to repeat the activity a few minutes later. The newly hauled seal cautiously approaches the nearest group of hauled seals and sniffs one of them, which invariably jumps a mile and turns to growl its disapproval of such a rude and sudden awakening. Should the newly hauled seal settle too close and in the personal space of another seal, it will be swatted repeatedly by the fore-flipper of the established seal, as well as being howled at to say, 'Get out of my face!' Once it is sure it is safe to do so, the new arrival finds a suitable and comfortable spot and starts to snooze; but it wakes up frequently to perform a visual check of its surroundings before settling back to sleep.

Disturbed seals stampeding to the sea

- *Returning to the sea:* The manner in which a seal returns to the sea depends on its location in relation to the sea and its mood. Some appear to make a sudden decision to head seawards, others resist the inevitable for as long as they can, before finally taking the plunge. Occasionally, seals that have hauled out at high tide get marooned well above the waterline when they re-awake at low tide. These seals may panic, when a route back to the sea is not obvious or involves a steep drop. High dives have been known, as have earth-shattering belly-flops as seals land in shallow rock pools, and these can be distressing to watch. Other seals become increasingly wet as the tide rises over them, and may even use their claws and body friction to hang on as long as possible. Those on offshore rock skerries in a calm sea may even appear to be resting on the water's surface as a rising tide encroaches, only to be floated off when their buoyancy can be resisted no longer.

Seal Stories

Chairlift

'Chairlift' is a very special seal, and one of my top favourites (I have rather a lot of them!). He was the first seal to be added to my photo-identification catalogue back in June 2000. He is named after a pattern on the right side of his neck, which to me looks like a button ski lift, that no-one else seems able to 'see'. Needless to say, I get a lot of stick for Chair-

'Chairlift' yawning

lift's name. When I first met Chairlift, he was probably around two or three years old, and a bit girly looking. I have had the unrivalled privilege of watching him grow up in his natural environment. As a juvenile, Chairlift loved playing in the shallows with other seals. As he hit adolescence, he spent hours play-fighting with other male seals of a similar age, such as 'Lighthouse' and '23', but this resembled handbags at dawn, and he has been known to fall asleep mid-bout, with his head resting on his opponent's neck, only to resume sparring again when they wake from their snooze. Chairlift was the first seal that I saw over 100 times, but now five other seals have overtaken him in the sightings race. Most of his visits were during the moulting and breeding seasons, but as he's got older, he has visited less frequently. As he hit ten or 11 years old, Chairlift only visited during the foraging season, so he might have been off trying his luck at being a beachmaster elsewhere. More recent sightings suggest he has given up on this idea, as last year he was seen during the foraging and breeding season. I've watched him in a variety of locations, and while he loves sleeping and rolling his head around in exaggerated yawns, he is also a very active seal, though I have never seen him being aggressive towards other seals, despite the fact that he is now a mature adult in the prime of his life. For seals that don't get to pass on their genes, perhaps this is their lot: Chairlift seems to be a very contented seal and, if it is possible, he is a seal with a very kindly face – not one covered with battle scars!

Wriggle

Of all the pups I have observed over the years, Wriggle's first delighted me the most. 'Wriggle' is a beautiful adult female seal, although a very distinctive scar above her right eye gives her a constantly surprised look on one side! She chose to have her first pup in a good viewing spot; it was the most gorgeous-looking fluffy pup that we called 'Bubbles'. I began watching Bubbles' development on day 1, and was able to see her first feed. I was quite anxious when, a week later, Wriggle decided to take Bubbles for a swim. During a feed, Wriggle moved her body and hauled down to the water's edge, forcing her hungry pup to follow. As soon as her pup latched on again, Wriggle moved into the water and Bubbles followed, only to be rolled over by the small breakers. It was an anxious time, but Wriggle kept very close to her pup, even encouraging Bubbles to put her head un-

'Wriggle'

derwater for the first time. As Bubbles got the hang of swimming, she and her mother had some very tender moments together, appearing to kiss nose to nose on several occasions. After a short while, Wriggle decided to bring Bubbles back to shore, but they got separated by a very large wave. Wriggle could be seen raising her head clear of the water to search for her pup, whom she found safe and sound, and then both returned to the beach to resume the feed. A week later, it was all change. No longer was Wriggle in charge of feeds! Bubbles did not want to get wet, and when Wriggle tried the same trick, Bubbles refused to follow. In fact, this time, Bubbles forced her mother to follow her further and further up the beach to feed. As soon as Bubbles latched on, we could see the reason why, as a big wave lapped right behind Bubbles' rear flippers. Even at such a young age, it seemed Bubbles had an instinctive knowledge about how far up the beach the next wave would reach. Wriggle weaned her pup after the maximum lactation period of 21 days, after which both of them disappeared from the cove. Despite being seen, Wriggle didn't pup again for another four years. That October she was photographed by Dave Mc-Bride on the Isles of Scilly, looking sufficiently fat to be pregnant. By October, she was back in Cornwall, and early that month gave birth to her second pup, 'Seaspray'. It was interesting to learn that as a breeding female, Wriggle had arrived from a westerly direction to pup on the north Cornish coast.

A pregnant 'Ghost 2', three days before giving birth to her pup

Ghost 2

Early one September, Rob Jutsum was taking a short break in north Devon, and he photographed a small collection of seals hauled out on rock ledges. Interested to learn more, he sent his photos to Devon Biodiversity Records Centre, which forwarded them to me, as Rob had questions about one seal in particular. Immediately, I realized I knew the female, as she had had her pup on the north Cornish coast the year before. Females that pup here are rarely seen during the moulting and foraging

seasons, so it has always been a mystery where they spend the rest of their year. I waited in anticipation at my local patch for 'Ghost 2' to turn up, and was delighted and amazed when 12 days later she appeared right on cue, looking heavily pregnant, and had her pup three days after that. Ghost 2 had been hauled out on spiky rocks in north Devon; had completed a journey of over 100 miles carrying her pup, only to haul out over another boulder beach. She successfully weaned this pup, named 'Rocky' from his location, despite him getting into endless scrapes – trapped between boulders, sneaking behind his mother's back into big breakers, and ending up on a different part of the beach altogether. Since this momentous occasion, Ghost 2 has returned again to have her third pup in three years, which she gave birth to inside a cave accessed via a small vertical slit in the cliffs. Our seal mothers really are incredibly resilient. After learning that Wriggle had swum in to pup from a westerly direction, it was interesting to know that Ghost 2 had arrived from the opposite direction.

Beachmaster W

The first seal I ever photographed mating turned out to be W – only identifiable from a small, W-shaped scar down on his right thigh. I hadn't recognized W at the time, but did so three years later, a year after he had become the established dominant male, or beachmaster, on the breeding beach. W was not the largest male seal on the beach; in fact, he had few distinctive features. Yet somehow he was able to stamp his authority across the breeding beach with just one look. He reigned supreme for five years, having only one really serious scrap, which left only a slight scar on the top of his back. He took his beachmaster duties very seriously once there were two pups on the breeding beach – it seems mating with only one female wasn't worth exerting his energy for!

Beachmaster 'W'. The distinctive scar on his thigh (top); mating (above)

The sixth year, however, despite turning up in September at the start of the breeding season, he disappeared after less than a week, and we feared he had been ousted by a younger and stronger adult male. From that point on, there was a succession of new beachmasters, each lasting just a few days. The lack of strong leadership on the breeding beach caused anarchy, with males regularly scrapping with each other, disturbing all the other seals. How we longed for the return of W; we hadn't realized what a strong and calming influence he'd had on the others. Much to our relief, W did come back at the end of November. He looked fit and well, but was a shadow of his former self. He skulked up the beach under the camouflage of the cliff, only moving when the incumbent beachmaster wasn't looking. He got about half way up the beach, but the moment W and the beachmaster made eye contact from over 100 m, W was off, hurtling back to the sea. He had lost his confidence, and with it his control of the breeding beach. We hope he will enjoy his retirement and achieve the level of contentment exhibited by non-breeding males like Chairlift.

'Medallion Man'

Medallion Man

'Medallion Man' was first identified at a wild seal haul-out at around four years old. Since then, he has developed a taste for life in harbours – Newquay Harbour to be specific. Seals are intelligent creatures, and Medallion Man learned of the easy pickings to be had around active fishing harbours. Fish discards probably lure seals into harbours in the first place. People on trip boats are always delighted to see seals, and those who have been out on leisure fishing cruises can often be persuaded to part with a few fish on their return to harbour… so begins a life of habituated humanized behaviour likely to last the seal's lifetime. Seals that spend any time in harbours are exposed to a whole new range of threats, ranging from the superficial – algal growth on their backs – to the much more serious and potentially life-threatening – propeller wounds; getting hooked in anglers' line, or the ingestion of light-grade diesel fuel. Fortunately, Medallion Man spends only a short time hanging around Newquay harbour before returning to the wild seal haul-outs. We hope he doesn't follow the example of another seal, 'Superman', who spent four years commuting between Newquay harbour and the wild seal haul-outs before disappearing, never to be seen again.

Puffa, the rehabilitated seal

'Puffa' was rescued from Sennen Cove at the age of a week and a half, still with her white coat, despite being well fed and fat. On high spring tides and rough seas, Puffa may have been washed out of her birthing site escorted by her mother, or she had become separated from mother. Either way, as Puffa had been handled by humans who were trying to be helpful, the Seal Sanctuary Animal Care Team had little choice but to rescue her from a beach that had a lot of human activity. During her clinical assessment, it was discovered that Puffa had an infected nail-bed, so she was given antibiotics and the middle claw on her right fore-flipper was removed. After a successful convalescence and reintegration with the resident adult seals at Gweek, Puffa was released less than six months later at Gunwalloe. Twenty-one months after that, Puffa was identified at a north coast haul-out where the yellow flipper tag 079 on her right rear flipper was photographed. A regular visitor to this site, Puffa has been seen every year since. At five years old, Puffa was looking heavily pregnant, although she must have had her pup in a sensibly secret location. The following year, Puffa gave birth at an open beach site, and although the birth wasn't seen, it was heard, alerting everyone to the new arrival — a very

'Puffa', aged 5 years and 2 months

bemused-looking pup we called 'Puffling'. It has been wonderful to watch a rehabilitated seal behaving like all the other wild seals, and breeding success is the ultimate indicator of this, strengthening Puffa's place as a firm favourite with Seal Sanctuary staff and Cornwall Seal Group members alike.

Threats to Grey Seals in Cornwall... and what we can do to help them

Survival in the open ocean and around our coast is tough, and even helpless-looking seal pups must be born hardy. Huge storms whip our seas into tumultuous peaks and deep abysses. Breakers relentlessly pound our shores, energized by gigantic Atlantic swells, sometimes for weeks on end. Low tides provide some respite, but at high tide most seals are forced to take their chances at sea. Small pups still with muscles to develop can tire quickly, and on quiet days after a lengthy winter storm, many calls are made to the British Divers Marine Life Rescue Hotline by people concerned about pups they have seen. Each call is followed up, and pups have been found with broken limbs, broken jaws and smashed skulls. Such is the harshness of nature.

More frustrating are the seals found with avoidable conditions, often as a result of human interaction. One of the most gruesome photographs I have received was of a juvenile seal with an open wound down half of the left side of its face, thought to have been caused by a boat strike.

Marine litter: on beach (left); on seal haul-out (right)

A seal with a packing band

Marine litter can be found on any beach, in varying quantities, but the beach morphology inevitably accumulates more rubbish in some areas than others, sometimes trapping it for months on end. Playful and curious creatures, seals are unable to resist exploring something unusual in the water, and have been seen eating floating crisp packets and dragging durable plastic sacks underwater, only to surface in a panic, as the plastic has broken leaving a piece wrapped around a tooth. Worse still, a beautiful, white-coated seal pup swam head-first into a see-through plastic bag floating just beneath the surface. Seals are erratic breathers, so at first this merely presented a challenge against which to swim, but as the pup tried to take its first breath, its panic was visible. After a few seconds, the pup had the intelligence to reverse, and was fortunate to lose its suffocating mask.

'Splash' surrounded by plastic bottles

'Splash' was the only white-coated pup that I have watched who loved going in the sea almost from birth. He would be seen swimming just offshore, with his mother in close attendance on most days, and his pleasure was ob-

vious to see. But during one particularly high tide, I had to endure watching Splash struggling to keep afloat at the back of his birthing zawn (a deep, narrow sea inlet), his mother anxiously trying to protect him by using her body to break up the worst of the waves. As Splash was tumbled by the 'washing machine' effect of the sea, he was repeatedly hit by the plastic bottles, an oil drum and a plank of wood that had all been funnelled up by the force of the water into the zawn. This was such a distressing experience, as at the time I had no idea whether Splash would survive his battering or not. Fortunately, as the tide receded, Splash's ordeal came to an end, and he lived to fight another day.

During numerous beach cleans, fishing gear and storm-damaged or discarded net are the main materials collected. Over 100 different live seals in Cornwall and the Isles of Scilly have been photographed with some form of net entanglement, with live net entanglement rates being between 3 and 5 per cent of all seals seen, most seals becoming entangled while swimming in and around floating rafts of ghost net. An unknown number of seals drown as a result of becoming entangled in long lengths of underwater net too heavy to drag to the surface. Seal teeth are not designed for biting their way out of nets, and

Net-entangled male (left). 'Netttie', trapped in a trawl net (right). 'Kettle' showing the damage caused by being caught in a trawl net (below right)

attempts to do so would result in severely cut gums. Most net entanglement of live seals occurs in monofilament, and around two-thirds of injuries are serious and potentially life-threatening. Despite this, seals survive a surprisingly long time (up to seven years) with these horrific and presumably painful injuries. Small seals are most at risk, as they have a lot of growing to do into a net of fixed diameter. Juveniles are easier to catch and immobilize, so rescue efforts are more practically focused on relieving these seals of their scarves or shawls of net.

Unlike our other marine mammals, seals are exposed to a range of different human effects when hauled out on land. Here seals are vulnerable to a range of human distur-

Left to right: The disturbed seal looks at you… moves towards the water… enters the sea

bance that affects their energy budget, compromising their nutritional state. Disturbing a hauled-out seal reduces the amount of energy the seal can get from digesting its food, at the same time as using more energy to move into the sea and out again. So, disturbing a seal during its digestion break is like a double whammy to its energy budget. Repeated disturbance by humans can be as high as eight times in one hour, which is likely to seriously compromise a seal's nutritional status. Disturbance is a complex issue, dependent on the individual seal, prevailing wind conditions, the level of natural ambient sound from the wind and waves, and the familiarity of the location to the seal. In the first instance, a seal's attention is likely to be attracted by hearing a sound (high-pitched, excited voices or dog barks), or smelling something unfamiliar, such as people. If, as a seal looks up, it sees something unusual that is perceived as a threat, the seal is likely to move. If the danger stimulus disappears, the seal may resettle; if not, the seal is likely to return to the safety of the sea. The best way to avoid disturbing seals is to be quiet, move slowly, keep a low profile, keep your distance, and observe the seal's reactions to you. If it looks at you, you are already close enough, and any closer movement will result in the seal returning to the sea in a compromised state. General advice is that 100 m is close enough to approach a hauled-out seal, which is a great range from which to observe seals through binoculars or a telescope. The three stages of disturbance are: (1) The seal looks at you; (2) The seal moves towards the water, and (3) The seal enters the sea.

Any seal rushing towards the sea has been disturbed. During the moulting season, with

Claws missing (above). Pregnant female (right)

blood close to the surface of the skin, disturbance can increase heat loss and upset a seal's thermal balance. During the breeding season, the consequences of disturbance can be even more serious. A pregnant mother carries her pup in her lower abdomen. If disturbed, she may rush over sharp boulders to the safety of the sea, causing untold damage to her unborn pup. Common injuries caused by disturbance are gashed bellies and claws ripped out as they get trapped between boulders. With a little knowledge and care, most seal disturbance can be avoided, leaving the seals to sleep in peace, for everyone to enjoy watching.

Seals that visit Cornwall's harbours face additional threats – from the obvious, such as propeller wounds, to the less obvious of ingesting light-grade diesel fuel oil. Possibly the greatest risk to seals is our love of ani-

Begging for food from a boat (above). Being fed mackerel (left)

mals and desire to get close and interact with them. Feeding seals that are begging for food can lead them into a lifetime of humanized behaviour in a very dangerous environment. Feeding seals from and around boats, links boats and food in a seal's mind. During the winter, the only boats leaving the harbour are likely to be fishing boats, around which seals are unwelcome visitors. Please learn from human experience with gulls, which are now considered a pest by some. Never feed wild seals, however much they beg.

Seals and People

A seal rescue

Routine survey work can turn out to be anything other than routine, if one of the seals on the haul-out turns out to be a six-month-old entangled in monofilament net. So many factors must be considered before taking the decision to rescue a seal, and the safety of the rescuers is paramount. Not all seals observed in net can be rescued, but one of the lucky ones was 'Myrtle'. All rescues are co-ordinated by British Divers Marine Life Rescue in collaboration with the National Seal Sanctuary at Gweek, or, if the Sanctuary is full, the RSPCA Wildlife Centre at West Hatch.

The tide was coming in, and the seal's position meant a rescue needed to be swift to stand any chance of success. Access to remote beaches can be hazardous, and for Myrtle's rescue a rope safety team was needed. After scaling the precipitous slopes, the seal rescue team of three made it to the beach without being spotted by Myrtle – had she heard or seen them,

A rescued seal, 'Myrtle' (top), and the net that was removed from around her neck (above)

The rescue of 'Myrtle'

she would have bolted for the sea, and all the rescuers' efforts would have been in vain. Using the cover of rocks for as long as possible, the two most experienced seal handlers, Dan and Tim, made their way across the open beach in a crouched position until Myrtle finally lifted her head and spotted them. In no time at all, Myrtle had turned around and shot off for the sea. Had she not had a split second's indecision about which of two routes to take, she would have escaped, but her slight delay gave Dan and Tim the time they needed to spring into action, sprinting towards the seal and catching her in the shallows. Dan launched himself at Myrtle, and as Tim and Rob arrived, they were able to immobilize her and take her to drier land. After assessing Myrtle's wounds, they removed the net tightly encircling her neck, but her deep wounds needed treatment, so the decision was made to take her to Gweek.

The rescue of 'Myrtle'

Hauling any seal up the cliff is tough work, and Myrtle weighed in at a hefty 31.5 kg, taking the strength of all five rescuers to pulley her to the cliff top. The experienced Animal Care Team at Gweek are used to nursing seals with this kind of injury back to health, so in three short weeks Myrtle was healed and ready to return to the wild, and just over a month later she was spotted fit, well and fat back at the wild seal haulout having been given a second chance, doing all the things that normal seals do – chasing around, playing and having fun!

Nearly all seals that have been rehabilitated at one of the many seal rescue centres around the UK are given a coloured rear-flipper tag with a unique reference number. Virtually all the seals being cared for at Gweek have been rescued in Cornwall, and are released back in Cornish waters. Reporting any tags

Residents of the National Seal Sanctuary, Gweek (above). Flipper tags (left)

you see, their colour, which side they were on, and the reference number really helps us to understand seal movements. Frequently, rehabilitated seals are accused of hanging around in harbours and fishing nets, but our evidence demonstrates this is not so.

Seal release

What to do if you see…

- *A white-coated seal pup, that is likely to be dependent on its mother.* Please don't touch the pup – as much for your safety as that of the pup. Contact the National Seal Sanctuary on 01326 221361, or British Divers Marine Life Rescue on their 24-hour hotline, 01825 765546. Retreat to a safe distance and observe the pup from a place where you can't be seen by either the pup or its mother, who may be in the sea waiting until the coast is clear to return to feed it. Trained medics or staff will be dispatched to your location as soon as possible.

- *A net-entangled, injured, visibly thin or unwell seal.* Please remember that if you scare this seal into the sea, rescuers are unlikely to be able to capture or help it. Please ring the National Seal Sanctuary on 01326 221361, or British Divers Marine Life Rescue on their 24-hour hotline, 01825 765546, and again retreat to a safe distance from where you can observe the pup from a place where you can't be seen.

- *A dead seal.* We can probably learn as much, if not more, about live seals from dead seals! Please call the Cornwall Wildlife Trust's Marine Strandings Network on 0345 201 2626, and they will send out trained volunteers to take photos, detailed measurements and records about the seal. While there is currently no funding for seal post-mortems, a few are done each year on cases where the cause of death is unclear.

- *All seal sightings.* Please email all your seal sightings to sue@cornwallsealgroup.co.uk

Photo-identification research findings

Detailed surveys and photo-identification have been carried out since 2000 at an index site – one of the two key seal haul-out sites on the north Cornish coast. There have always been two major seal haul-outs on the north Cornish coast, but not always in the same locations. From this index site, we have learned that seal numbers vary considerably on a monthly basis, with two peaks in numbers – the biggest during the moulting season, and a secondary peak in the breeding season. Examples of seals of known different ages have been photographed, and at least 800 different individual seals have been photographed here for a photo-identification catalogue. In 2006–9, each year between 215 and 357 different seals were identified visiting this site during the year, and with an identification rate of around 30 per cent of seals observed at any one time, we can assume the site is used by a lot more different individual seals than this. No seals are thought to be resident at this site all the year – only 2–10 per cent of identified seals visiting in any one year may be classified as semi-resident (seen more than 20 times a year); 31–37 per cent as regulars (visiting 5–19 times a year), and by far the greatest proportion (55–66 per cent of all those identified) are migrants – passing through and visiting the site less than five times a year. Ninety-two seals photographed at this index site have been photo-identified at 22 other sites around the South West, from Lundy and the north Devon coast west to the Isles of Scilly, and east along the south Cornish coast to Looe. Two seal movements that demonstrate the kind of routine journeys that seals make include 'Seahorse', an adult male which travelled from the St Ives area to Newquay and back in 12 days, and a second adult male that swam from mainland Cornwall to the Isles of Scilly and back in around 12 days. If we have learned anything about Cornwall's grey seals, it is that there is still much to learn, and that by collaborating with a range of organizations we learn most!

Canvey

Rescued in 1996, and rehabilitated at the National Seal Sanctuary at Gweek, 'Canvey' was released back into the wild a few months later. Between 2000 and February 2006, Canvey was seen just once a year at the index site, despite being an easily recognizable seal. In September 2006, aged ten years, Canvey

Sites on the Isles of Scilly, Cornwall and Devon coasts linked by seal movements

was recorded dead in Porthleven by Caroline Curtis, a Cornwall Wildlife Trust Marine Strandings Network volunteer. From cradle to grave, Canvey had been monitored, yet we still know so little about where he spent the bulk of his life, and while his death provided closure, it posed more questions than it provided answers!

I have found my niche in life. I love grey seals – they are what I am here for! Someone has to do this work and help to provide a voice for grey seals in a natural world shaped by human decisions.

Organizations and Groups

British Divers Marine Life Rescue
T: 01825 765546; http://www.bdmlr.org.uk

Cornwall Seal Group
T: 01736 754562; www.cornwallsealgroup.co.uk

Cornwall Wildlife Trust
T: 01872 273939;
http://www.cornwallwildlifetrust.org.uk

Cornwall Wildlife Trust's Marine Strandings Network
T: 0345 201 2626; http://www.cwtstrandings.org

The National Seal Sanctuary, Gweek
T: 01326 221361;
http://www.sealsanctuary.co.uk/corn1.html

The National Trust
http://www.nationaltrust.org.uk

RSPCA West Hatch Wildlife Centre
T: 0300 1234999;
http://www.rspca-westhatch-wildlifecentre.co.uk

Useful Websites

Seal photography
http://www.cornishseals.co.uk

Seal Preservation Action Group
http://www.sealaction.org

Seals Protection Groups
http://www.protectourseals.org.uk

Save our Seals Fund
http://www.saveoursealsfund.org

Tara Seal Research
http://www.sealresearch.org

Joint Nature Conservancy Council
http://www.jncc.gov.uk

References and Other Useful Books

Anderson, Sheila (1990), *Seals*, Whittet Books
Bonner, W. Nigel (1989), *The Natural History of Seals*, Christopher Helm
Westcott, Stephen (1997), *Grey Seals of the West Country*, Cornwall Wildlife Trust

Joint Nature Conservancy Council (JNCC) (2008), *Marine Monitoring Guidance*
Sea Mammal Research Unit (SMRU) (2002), *Seal diet factsheet*
SMRU (2008), *Scientific Advice on Matters Related to the Management of Seal Populations*
SMRU (2009), *Seals like it hot*
Cornwall Seal Group and Exeter University, Tremough (2007–9), *Grey Seals of Cornwall and the Isles of Scilly Census*
Cornwall Seal Group (2009), *Entanglement of grey seals at a haul out site in Cornwall, UK*
Annual reports of the Cornwall Seal Group, 2005–9